Thoughts of a Teenager

By

Donald R. Thompson II

ISBN 978-0-6152-1787-1

I would like to thank God for all he has done for me and continues to do in his will. I would also like to dedicate this book, my first and hopefully not my last, to my family and friends because without them I would have long since met my end.

Introduction

During the small steps I took through my last few years I have learned a couple lessons. #1 take it easy when things do not go your way because only patience can bring an end to a bad day. #2 only worry about you until you are through because you cannot jump in to save them if you know you cannot swim. #3 and the most important one to me, is that the world is what we make it, whether we like or not and with a little hard work the earth could be our favorite spot. Now do not let me confuse you, these poems have little to do with teaching life lessons. As a matter of fact they were created for simple enjoyment whether you are in times of grief and pain, happiness, joy, love or sorrow. I am sure you will find a poem to read today that you will still like tomorrow. Again I do not intend to bore, teach or impose! These poems are just some thoughts of a teenager you may or may not know.

Table of Contents

Despair (tribute to the trail of tears)

I hear her call in my ear,
and for her safety I shall fear.
Hunted down like a wild deer,
their force pierced her heart like a spear.
Her pain and her screams somewhere near,
ran through my veins and rang through my ears.
Some how I hope she will make it here.
So her voice can drown the white man's cheers.
Though I pray their voice caused her no tears!

As I walk with my tribesmen in the arid air,
I wonder why Mr. Jackson was so unfair,
taking us far, far away from where,
the water, earth, and sun would share,
the pleasures of life like the graceful mare,
and then through the bushes faith prepared,
a surprise reunion with my eternal pair.
The love of my life was just standing there,
at the edge of a river just floating there,
with her cool brown skin and long black hair.
Suddenly she became a small glare,
and my body slumped with exhaustion under heavy air.
Then I died a painful death from my tribe's despair.

Love

The caring voice of mother in the cold heavy rain,
warms my heart like breath to a window pane.
Her perfect cooking just drives me insane.
And the way she helps soothe my pain,
sends my body soaring like a choo-choo train.
She always protects me.
Just like any mother to her baby,
she cares for me to death,
watching, helping even after her last breath,
mysterious like the God above
is my guardian angel, a mother's love.

Beauty

Slim, trim, divine
Is the girl whom I call fine!
Her body an endless curved line
Sends chills straight through my spine
In my head I wish she was mine
In a world of joy and endless time
Her warm brown skin and long black hair
So soft and dreamy, makes me float on air
That tight black dress with those killer heels
Gives off a strong body language that I can feel
The one and only taken out of my dreams
She is the hottie, the cuttie or so it seems
But then physical beauty runs only skin deep through the seams
Then again her image is so intoxicating
Tempting me forever more to stop waiting
To get up and ask would you be mine
Because you are so fine
Like a beautiful glass of white wine.
Or like my rose garden around nine.
When the stars brightly shine,
Like your eyes on the dark green vines
O, beautiful would you be mine?

Friends

When there is no one to look to
To help you get through
All the troubles of life you are going through
Just remember the one who takes away all the strife
Not a husband, girlfriend, boyfriend, wife
But your best friend whose love is larger than life

Your umbrella to keep off the rain
The relaxing spa that soothe your pain.
A friend's comfort shall never wane
And their will is strong enough to stop a train.
Nothing in the world could be a better gain
Then the trust and understanding of the kid down the lane.

Valentine

The candy, balloons, and sweet black rose
Hidden from her so she will not know
The one she loves, cares more than he shows.
For a whole year he saved every penny he earned
Dreaming of the gift he would buy as he tossed and turned
Always waking up to her undying passion that burned
In his heart.
Then came the day he thought they could never be apart.
He walked to the place where they were suppose to meet
Than he sat down to rest his feet
And right before nine
Shots rang out and one hit him from behind
Leaving him dead for his girlfriend to find
But on the silver chain was a message so kind
It said "I will always love you my valentine"

Music

The sweet, strong flow of the sax downtown
Flows through the air and gently surrounds,
The people of the night life making their rounds.
No one knows where it comes from that lovely sax sound..
It slowly drowns the howl of the barking hounds
While giving new energy to runners trying to lose some pounds.
Who plays this sax and gives life to the still dark air?
Why its just old man Jenkins and his dancing cats
Swaying to the rhythm of Jenkins' new sax!

Rejection

Far from perfect and scarred for life
He is the one they say will never have a wife.
The poor kid is so smart and so nice
But for some reason the girls will never look twice
Maybe its the smell, the clothes, or the mice
Or the fact that he can never reach her price.
He wonders why people called him nasty when he played with his lice
I guess maybe there is just one who has to be rejected
Or maybe mom and dad never saw it coming
Or maybe they just couldn't do anything!

Cast Away (Rejection 2)

In the corner, all alone, in his zone
His world, no joy, no love, no girl
His hopes washed away like dirt in the rain
Its sad to say his life took this turn
After all he had going for him
He just crashed and burned
It all started with her at school
He was young still young, but now also a fool
Because he cheated his girl
By sleeping with Dru
When his girl heard the news her little heart was torn
Anger fueled her and rage took the place of her love
She told him "no more" as she yelled her scorn
Asking for strength and help from above, to move on
She left him and so did Dru
After all what happened last night was through
Leaving the dumb-founded boy in a new abyss
Created from corruption and despair
He thought to himself "It can't get any worst than this"
And he walked off as if he didn't care.
Yet more trouble loomed around the corner for him
For word had spread to his coach in the gym
That he was doing drugs and his good grades were slim?
When coach ran into him later that day
And told the boy his scholarship had been thrown away,
Again the boy was cast into darkness
His life now only full of emptiness
No joy, no love, no girl
No money, all alone in a shattered world...

... As the year progressed, the boy lost what little
he still possessed
when Dru announced she was three months pregnant
one by one his friends disappeared
even his parents got tired of his tears
they threw him out onto the street
nowhere to go or sleep and nothing to eat
just a torn heart and the shoes on his feet.
Where the boy is today, I don't know
But best of luck and all hope to him
To get himself back together, because I do know
Rain, shine, wind, sleet, not even snow

Will stop him from making sure
That no one leaves him any more!
Black Rose

If I had one for every girl on the globe
I would give them a sweet black rose
Unique is its beauty and everyone knows
The sweet fragrance can charm any nose.

Why the girl herself is so much like a rose
Nothing less than fine from her head to her toes
And those sparkling teeth like soft petals in a row
Shine like her hair, the strands combining into a single flow

Why if I had a rose
For every girl on the globe
I'd give each girl one because everyone knows
A rose is a rose
But in the light of your perfection
Love, like a rose just has to grow.

The Cheater

Mary thought he was trying to please her
With the gifts like the candy and pink furs
But he was just hiding behind his secret store
Of crimes, cheating, and playing galore!

Then one night while he was in the shower
His cell rang by the bed at half past the hour
It was his so called "client" waiting for him at a tower
Her heart snapped in two and her love turned sour.

She followed him to the tower to see this client
And for the first few moments she was calm and silent
But when they started kissing she could not hold it in
She ran over and began punching her in the chin
And had the client limping in a dress so short and thin
And then Mary turned to her man and said
"you little cheater this relationship has just came to an end."

Fear

Silent, cold and dark is this house I fear
Inside only moans, groans, and creaks will you hear.
In the halls lonely knights stand with their spears
While starring pictures shed bloody tears.

I try to walk silently down the hall
Chasing the moving shadows along the wall
just when they stop my phone gets a call
but then my house never had any power at all
And my phone line had been cut last week with a saw

Nevertheless I pick up the phone and say hello
And the voice that replied was far from mellow
Its dark, nefarious whisper turned my body to jello
And then my heart stops and I drop to the floor
As my worst fear walks out the door.

Death

Her body cold, limp and pale makes no sound
While her blood seeps through the wound and to the ground
When she was spotted, the weapon nor the predator could be found
The police search high and low around the town
But still no weapon or predator could be found.

No one said they saw her or heard her screams
And most of the town was sleeping with sweet dreams
While the cold murderer drives off in low beams
Making a clean get away or so it seemed
For his car ran out of control and flew over the rail beams
Sending his body into the river's dangerous and silent streams

So on that day both victim and murderer met their death
But no one knows exactly what happened that day
Because now the only witnesses draw no breath
As they rest in coffins side by side, day by day
Forever in them the secret of death lays.

Pain (greed)

Caused by the man's quest for his greedy gain
His welts seep and bleed from pain
They burn and sting in the warm summer rain
But yet the whip keeps coming fast like a train
In his mind he asks himself "am I insane?"
"to let this suffering go on and never wane"
Is money worth all this
Is money something I will surely miss
Or will I worry more for my lover's kiss
As the cuts grow deeper like an abyss
The insuperable pain binds his hands by the wrist
"will I escape from this
this pain from sin of avarice?"

Peace

When will it stop
The pain and suffering must come to an end
No more shooting and killing friends
It is time to act as women and men
Instead of letting go when hope is thin
Do something to save the future of the children
Because without the help of everyone they cannot win
Without the help, history will repeat itself again
We cannot allow a world war three to happen
Control the anger and jealousy that burns within

The power belongs to those who try to grasp it
So take the power and push yourself past the limit
Because peace will only come to this earth if everyone wants it

The earth is in the hands of the people
We can either drop it and break it's spine
Or lift it up towards the sun to shine!

Sad Boy

In the corner of the room at school by the water pail
Sits a little boy who cries and wails
The people just watch as his sad tears fell
But the boy never stopped crying until the sound of the bell
At home he watched the rain drops from his stairwell
In his mind resonates the screams and yells
Turning his cherry red face a deadly pale
What troubles the boy he'll never tell
He just sits by the tombstone waiting for her to come back
But all that's left are some pictures and the memory of having to dress in black.

Bojangles

Everyday when I wake up in the morning
There is nothing to eat and my stomach is groaning
So where to go to get my breakfast munchings?

Then it hits me go to bojangles to get a fresh biscuit
Because they serve em hot, fresh, and quick
So I go through the drive-thru in my new whip
Order some coffee and two boberry biscuits
I eat in the lot then off to work I zip
But around twelve my stomach said "its time to quit"
So I leave for bojangles to take another pit
It was harder to choose something this time with my stomach in a fit
So I pick the buffalo bites which was the only window lit
And to make a short story real quick
If you want something to eat that's good but not light or whipped
Come in to bojangles for some of them famous chicken and biscuits.

Marlene

Here's good wishes to you on this special day
A memory I hope you'll be glad to replay
Please have fun and try to do things your way
Place yourself on the throne but just for today (and)
Yell to the crowd its your birthday

Be happy and joyful with your crazy smile
In the club have fun get loose and go wild
Run away from your troubles and play like a child
Til the sunrise of the next morning day trial
Here's cheers to a girl with that eighteen year style
Down with anything hot but not mild
A girl with that sweet black rose style
Yeah Marlene got em going wild

May the rest of your days be perfect and peaceful
And I wish success and a good life for you (because)
Real women like you are hard to find in a place so dull (so)
Live and be happy doing what you do (and)
Everyone one day will look up and say
Now Marlene is the person I want to be
Everyday in my own way because she knows how to be free!

Jealousy and Envy

The green monster that lives within
Caused by the want of what others win
The hard earned fame they wish to win
While rendering your success thin
Watch for them, their stench foul and green in the wind
Their mind set to create the new trend
And have the world revolve around them

Revenge

No time to cry, whine or pout
I must devise a plan like that of the count
They took away my purpose of life
My beautiful children and my lovely wife
Now it is time to give them strife
Revenge is my weapon to torture their souls
Little by little I'll take a part of their whole
When they have nothing left but some clothes
And when I reach the top of this world
Only then will I tell all to my foes
As they draw their last breath in this world
They will see how revenge knows
How to take from one and give the other the pearl

Life

The time of breath, joy and pain
The love, the games, and the summer rain
The hate, the sorrow in your mind clear and plain
Forever flowing like the blood in my veins
The brown sand of beaches and the waves that rise and wane
Soothe the body like a gentle mist on a window pane
And sends me to my idyllic world where I am sane
Where my friend stays just down the lane

Don't Quit

Get up and stop screaming
Cause you know you're not dreaming
This pain is real
As well as this bad ordeal
But you do not quit
Because you can ride past the limit

Stare at the roadblock face to face
Tell it to move away from your space
Then happily move on to those golden gates
Where the dreams are real and luxuries await
Because when you don't quit
Only you are the limit

The Harlem Renaissance

Around the nineteen twenties in Harlem City
Blacks came together showing their creativity
Their words, their music, and their souls so gracefully
Illustrated their struggle against white supremacy
From the words of Hughes and McKay that rhyme so gently
To the sweet flow of the "Duke's" Jazz sympathy
Even the angelic voice of little Miss Smith
Was enough to make you tap your feet or move your hips
This renaissance prospered through the hearts of the black people and their wits
There in the little city of Harlem was a hopeful light
Shining with the pride of a people's brilliant fight
No hands were ever raised in this nebulous plight
Just the breath taking beauty of the people
Who reach up for their rights!

Sing

As voice coalesces with rhythm and emotion,
A sound is born
A sound used to express a soul's devotion
Or a heart that is torn

A continuous flow aided by instruments
Or a charming melody that stands alone.

Success

Success is materials at their best
Whether its separate houses for your guests,
A different bed every night just to rest
With shoes and jewelry to match every dress
Or an army of maids to clean the mess.
Our world is a place working for success,
It is about having more instead of less.

Tobacco

Ladies and gentlemen, sisters and bros
Hold your applause and listen to my flow
As I tell you about the harmful substance tobacco
Every year as fifty million smokers inhale their raspy breath
Four hundred and fifty thousand meet their death
What's so bad about this stuff
Cigarettes, cigars, and snuff
They're just filled with thousands of chemicals
Two hundred of which are known poisons that kill
So why do some people think its cool
When smoking is liked drowning yourself in a pool
With all that arsenic
And house cleaners in the mix
If the silent mists of carbon monoxide doesn't put you in a fix
The acetone from nail polish ought to shut your lips
But if you really want something to chew
Or just don't have anything to do
Buy some candy and go outside, do a verb
And you will forget about puffing on some herb
I'm DT and poetry is my verb! Ya heard!

Destruction

Battlegrounds, graveyards, and deserted houses
A place where you either die or wear black pants and blouses
Hearts torn, widowed spouses mourn
From deaths of soldiers to innocent children
Who is responsible?
Who is to blame?
I'll tell you who!
The person who fights for no cause
The person who says it is our duty to help
And the person who sits and watches it all

Accident

Blood oozing down my severed leg
Trickling down the street towards the drain
With no one around to hear my shrieks of pain
I stop… to listen to the pitter patter
Of the dripping gashes that cover my head
Glass shards had done their harm
As I looked at the shredded skin of my arms
Pulsing headaches, a empty stomach,
And the feeling of someone hammering little spikes
Into every sinister inch of my body, all added
To the pain of my confusion.
Who am I?
Where am I?
Is that my car wrecked by the light?
Or was I a pedestrian who was hit
While walking at night?
Where is everyone?
Will anyone come to look for me here?
To help me?
To save me?

Payback

I see you now for what you really are!
I had everything I could ever want in life.
The condo, the pool, friends, and a car
Then you turn on me and take it all away.

Alright, I can play your game,
You took me from rags to riches and back again
But that's okay because your fame…
Is coming to an end

Watch your step and protect your back, because
From now on and it is hunting season
Just remember you gave me the reason to attack
To lash back

Hmm… yeah I'll give you a dose of your own
Medicine. Leave you with nothing
Cold, dark, and all alone
With no one to call to for help

And as you shriek and scream and lose your mind
You'll lose all grasp of reality
Asking why me? Only to find
That your greed became your own fatality

Jealousy

The designer jeans, silver chains and tims
He has it all and he always wins.
Smooth face, killer eyes and pearly whites too!
Can't help but hate as he passes through.
Who does he think he is walking like that, with a
Pimp walk strut, fat jeans sagging low
And to top it off, he talks to the girls real smooth and slow
Oh no! C'mon I can't take it everyday his cool
Makes the girls drool and he cancels out my fool
Then again who wouldn't want a man shaped like
Hercules, built ford tough, and enough money to
Buy the top dollar stuff?
I won't lie, I'm mad at ya!

Thanks Dad

For all the things you have done for us
All the cleaning, cooking, and putting up with our fuss
That must be hard to do without any sleep
Having to go to work until the sun's up and Brian's clock beeps
Everyone has a special day and today is yours, so
Remember as you relax and this father's day goes by
You are still the best dad ever in our eyes!

The Date

Its nine, the night is young and I have
just begun to amaze.
I cooked her favorite dinner, dimmed the lights
and set some candles ablaze.
Waiting for her to call, I play some music,
some smooth jazz to set the mood.
Then she rings, I answer, take her coat
and show her the way to the food.
I pull out her chair, complement her fine long
black hair, and told her to enjoy.
She grinned back at me like a child
receiving a new toy.
I could tell the food was good, it was still sizzling
hot like her little red dress,
that highlighted her whole body, an endless curved line,
nothing less than fine.
As she took another mouth watering bite, I thought
I was in heaven having her with me to dine.
We finished eating at about the same time
and for a while shared some old memories.
I told her how heart broken I became when we
went separate ways and she left me.
And the whole time I watched her gentle expression
and her soft, caring, brown eyes.
As she replied I'm sorry, I got myself together,
held out my hand and invited her to dance.
The cool moonlit night lasted for an eternity
as we glided across the floor.
Step after step, song after romantic song
every note, every melody brought her closer to me.
When she twirled away her dress did too. like a
velvet sea rising in the calm of a storm.
Then she would twirl back to me, I would dip
her, bringing my face inches to her rose petal lips.
She floated back up just in time for a slow dance.
She let me take full control as her delicate head
rested on my shoulder.
I held her just right by the waist, my heart
warmed by the glow of her flawless brown skin.
The night stood still with my goddess in my arms,

as we floated around the enchanted room without care or harm.
Eventually she grew sleepy and tired,
so i carried her upstairs to where we retired
in my master suite,
a room fit for my queen. A big cozy bed
garnished with a single black rose,
a painting of a sunset where the sea ebs and flows.
I placed her on one of my favorite fluffy pillows
and walked casually into the bathroom
and all its splendor, I stopped at the garden tub,
whose soothing earth tones almost matched hers.
I filled the tub with water, surrounding it with fragrant
scents and I turned the bubbles on low.
Then I told her, her spa was ready just take it
nice and slow.
Oh! It was torture to let that beautiful creature
go away, even for just an hour or so!
When she came out, her charming smile, her rosy cheeks,
her sexy body in her long black gown,
drove me mad, insane, just plain wild!
But we fell asleep only to wake up early at dawn.
I found myself surprisingly alone, my goddess was gone!
She wasn't in the bathroom, the ballroom, or down the hall,
nor was she in the dining room, I couldn't find her at all!
Was it real, was she ever here?
Here with me or was it a dream?
I ran back upstairs and bathed in the sun's golden beams
trying to grasp the reality of my recent past
then I saw it, a letter sealed with her gentle kiss
finally some proof at last of the girl I sorely miss.
I tore it open and read the contents:
"Thanks for the wonderful evening, I enjoyed
it so much! I loved the food, the dancing and your
gentle touch. I'm sorry I have to go but I'm a
busy girl you know. Yet I would like to do this again
for sure.
Yours Truly
Forevermore"

World Peace

This needs to stop
This living nightmare must come to an end
Silent, rotting corpses stacked one on top of another
Men tortured with vivid images of carnage
Images of a war started by the death of one man
Ignorant country declaring war to support a friend
Instead of punishing the man at fault who committed the sin
Images of a war started by the killing of one man
The support of allies linked like a food chain
Challenge one friend the others follow
The few countries that claimed neutral
Were assailed as bad as any other
U.S. loses their cool and declares war
After the sinking of many sisters and brothers
Images of a war fed on strength and deception
Hypocrisy of the highest demeanor
A president of a neutral country
Later declaring war
Then after celebrating galore
And falsely promoting war…
Says this needs to stop
A president with a dream
Images of a war that should never start
A league in which each country takes a part
A league said the president
Is exactly what we need
A league to make sure
Everyone gets fair a piece of the world
So then everyone in turn could experience world peace

Reflection

Thin fine black hair
Cool dark brown eyes
They say those are his eyes, his hair
My actions, my words, they say reflect his
Why had we been born together we would be twins.
So identical is his picture to mine
That I could use it as a mirror, small and fine

Leaders

Do you stand in front, or to the side?
Do you ask and answer or just hope for an answer?
Do you wait for a ride or do you prepare for the ride?
When they need you will you help or stare?

The door only opens to those who turn the handle
And light can only shine through the night,
When you take the time to light a candle
Only then will you find a future that is bright

Why Her?

She lays cold and limp with her bright red lips,
her complexion paler than the roses at her hips.
As the night transforms her grave dark and shady
A lonely husband mourns for his lady.
Why take her he asks?
An angel who wore a human mask.
How can an innocent girl who loved to spread joy,
Be abused and thrown away like a toy.
Deprived of life and breath
To spend eternity in the prison of death.

AP English IV

For an hour and a half more,
She wants us to read, write and discuss
We ask her, what do we need this class for?
"To improve your writing skills, now stop your fuss!
and share your thoughts on question four!"

After five minutes or more
The usual three star students reply
Securing their high grading score
While the other students give out a sigh
Because they did not read the night before
Every school day for a semester, no more
Each day was the same.

2006

We've spent four years together as a class,
through times rough as sand and smooth as glass.
Like the wind, I've seen people come and go.
Enemies hot as fire, friends gentle as snow.
We watched the changes as time progressed
as he matures and she gains finesse,
class after class we worked until we tired
slowly getting by as each day expired
with only the weekends to look forward to.
Images of wild parties lasting the night and through
the morning danced in our heads,
as we used our desks to sleep on like beds.
There were fights between enemies acting like they're ten
and unbelievable make-ups and sad break-ups between friends
but somehow we stayed together til the end,
anxiously awaiting for graduation to begin!
And as I look at those past four years,
so full of drama yet so dear,
I have but only two things to say.
To all my friends who I have here today
I want to thank you for your help
and let you know that I will never forget you.
And to the people I've grown to love so much,
know that no matter what I will always miss you!

Donald

Down to earth and always,
On the spot to help.
Never fear, I am your friend.
Always there until the end.
Like a warm soft bed, I
Do my best to comfort.

Orphan

The hustle and bustle of many feet
As people walk up and down the street,
As the wind howls and blows through my hair
The aroma of sizzling hot dogs float in the air.
The yellow sun dawns out in full bloom
Washing away a night of crime and gloom.
In the park joyful children play and play,
Waiting for their parents to come at the end of the day.
To take them to a nice warm home
Where love and comfort are free to roam.
How I wish to come home to such a place
Where I am welcome to live and stuff my face.
Sometimes I can taste the delicious food on the table.
As I gaze at the hot roaring fire, I am able
To imagine what it might feel like to have a family.
But in reality I have been alone for what seems an eternity.

Loving Pain

Her red lips soft as the petals of a rose
With her radiant skin she is a goddess at best.
Wearing the most intoxicating perfume to the nose,
Just one whiff put my heart to rest.

If I could have her for my own to keep
No treasures of precious metals could take her place!
But at last, when she walks by I weep
Because all I can settle for is a glance of her face.

It is a torture to see her beauty but never touch her skin
And her warm bright smile haunts through the day.
Every second, every dying minute, my heart grows thin.
Oh how love seems so unfair when it does not go your way

The lady of my dreams, perfection as a whole
If only I could have one kiss, I could rest my heavy soul!

Spring

Where is that season we call spring
A time filled with warm and joyous things
As the winds blow away and the trees start to bloom,
And the sunny days vanquish all the cold and gloom,
Little kids prepare for a break to play outside
While older boys and girls go on a ride
Maybe to the movies, to the mall, or to the beach
Anyplace where their parents are out of reach.
Spring! Spring! Spring! What a wonderful season.
When you can watch the clouds and let your mind escape reason.
I imagine new world's, new view, the future.
When spring comes, the past will be a blur
No more cold, icy snow days
Just the flowers blossoming in the month of May.

The Sea

An endless mass flowing into eternity
Sometimes shallow, sometimes deep and murky.
Supporter of life to those on land and in the deep.
Her gentle waves like a mother lull you to sleep.
But in a violent storm ships will toss and jerk
And when the gray clouds clear, no explanation will work
To express the deep dark secrets she hides beneath.
In the arctic north her waters freeze with grief
While towards the equator her colors are warm like her roofs.
From the fish who surface to hungry predators underneath,
In order to persevere in her dangerous waters of teal
Unsheathe your mind and remain determined and tranquil.

Spring

Birds, flap, fly, and sing
Flowers red, pink, and yellow
Feel the strong wind blow

Rainforest

The warm pond refreshes me
As I swing on the green jungle vines
Feel the tropical rain pour

My Mistress

Your devoting love is like a vortex pulling me down
Down into a lost paradise of ecstasy
Where you wait in your beautifully soft black gown.
Why your generous and angelic personality drives every girl's jealousy!

Here in your world white roses are spread all around
Making the flowers seem more like a carpet of cream cheese on the ground
Grrr!!! I screeched as I remember your touch.
And the way you were hugging me, oh how I miss you so much.

Night Fright

It was a dark and gloomy night.
In the black forest, the moon's pale light
only revealed the eyes of bodies hid from sight.
Here a small boy slowly walks home shivering with fright.
Hoping and praying with all his little might
That he would make it home to mom all right.
Floating along behind the boy was his blue kite
Which was torn by a tree on its first flight.
It took all day before he began to solve his plight.
Then up he climbed, through the branches high in the sky
Where the dark orange sun was setting in the corner of his eye.
The vibrant fall day grew old
And night emerged making him cold.
And as he slid down the oak tree with his kite.
The small boy slowly walked home, shivering with fright.
At home his mom hoped he would make it all right
But as she searched across the field, he was no where in sight.
Just a giant oak tree with all its might,
Standing tall with a blue gleam in the pale moon light

Remember...

Do you remember...
The timeless walks we took on the beach at night.
I remember...
The way your warm brown arms held me tight.

Do you remember...
The last time, your last walk.
I remember...
It happened just when you started to talk.

Do you remember...
The loud bang, then the shrieking pain.
I remember...
You sprawled out on the wet sand stained with blood and rain.

Do you remember...
Our farewell, your goodbye, me saying "don't die!"
I remember...
Your bright smile and your joyous spirit high as the sky!

Eert

With a little water, sun and air
He will grow big, brown, and tall with green waxy hair.
Standing tall and strong from the ground,
His canopy can be seen from miles around.
Yet when the wind blows through his many arms
He gently bends without care or alarm.
As each year goes on his hair turns yellow, brown, and red.
Towards the end of fall he becomes cold and dead.
Only to spring forward with new life in may.

Alone

I awake shivering to the darkness before dawn.
No good mornings or hellos, just a yawn.
I do what I need to in a few hours,
Brushing teeth and a tropical hot shower.
Still I remain by myself as I stroll through the hall,
The rest of them gently snoring could hear nothing at all.
I let the light clear the shadows as I enter the ghostly den
And while thinking of what to eat, I think of my friends
"will I see them, will they see me?" hmm… one may never know,
what will happen in life until that part of the show.
If my life is a show, then I am the audience.
Only I know all the twists and can make sense,
Of what they mean in the melting pot of my joys and sorrows,
Golden yesterdays, sad todays, and unknown tomorrows.
I am only myself, by myself, living for myself.
Whenever something goes wrong there is no one left
To shift the blame, point the finger elsewhere.
I am by myself, but I still care
For those outside my little carnival fair.
I try to love them and respect them all.
When they are down they can give me a call,
Tell me their problems, their rises and falls.
Their secrets forever safe in my world's silent halls.
But as I look at the mirror on the wall
I realize I am nothing more than what I saw…
Alone.

Poetry

I let words flow on paper and burn
In your mind.
Page after page you will turn
And deep emotions of the soul will you find.
I can engender an image of almost any scene,
Using rhyme to show what I mean.
All the poems I have written so far everyone enjoys.
Some poems make you happy like a brand new toy,
Others remind us of life and its sorrow,
While one may bring hope for a better tomorrow.
Either way I like writing poetry.
It gives me a way to express me.
All the good times and bad times
I have seen can be put into rhyme,
Accidents, awards, love and even crime.

Forever

One second, two second, three seconds, four
Forever goes on forever more.

From new to old to new again
The cycle of forever never ends.
Time without limit,
Eternity without bounds
Continuing without a sound.
Forever I wait for her,
Trying and trying
To make her stir.
Stir and awake to my presence
But forever I wait...

One second, two second, three seconds, four
Waiting on forever more.

Small trinkets I supply to show her I care.
I ask what she thinks
And she just gives a blank stare,
Then my heart sinks in a river of cold blood,
Throbbing, stinging from the pain of love.
Forever, I thought will it take to win her...

One second, two second, three seconds, four
A lonely heart mourns forever more.

A smile I finally win
And nothing more.
Oh how her beauty tortures so!
Yet for her love, I shall wait some more!

One second, two second, three seconds, four
A lonely lover weeps at fate's door.

I step my game up for another chance,
Hoping to change her mind with a little romance.
Yet again I try and try to win
But she turned me down yet again...

One second, two second, three seconds, four
A shattered heart tries to love once more.

By now, my friends wonder will I ever win?
It seems with each try my chances grow thin.
And as she walks by talking to her friends,
I thought now is the time for real magic to begin.
I planned out a date, a romantic night,
Hoping this evening would solve my plight.
And to my delight she said "sure".

One second, two second, three seconds, four
Will cupid's victim even the score?

I hope so, I thought as I rested my head.
"she did say sure but she also said
when she can find the time the date is on."
And since then, I have been listening to love songs…
Now I'm back…

One second, two second, three seconds, four
Life moves on forevermore.

Purple Rose

Hey this poem is just for you
Whenever you feel sad and blue.
Remember what I said...
"If I had one for every girl on the globe
I would give them each a sweet black rose"
... now listen to this instead.
You are no ordinary girl,
You take full command of your world.
Like your favorite color,
You are majestic showing honor and pride.
Whats more
Is that, you stay sweet with your smile opened wide.
Your funny jokes, your style and charm,
Makes me feel at ease and far from harm.
So I'm telling you and only you will know,
If I had just one and only one to show
How much I care.
I would give you your purple rose.
And like its beauty so fair
May our friendship end all despair!

Take a Break

If I could stop time
With my words, my rhyme...
I would take you wherever you want to go.

We can take...
Long walks at the beach to watch the waves eb and flow.

We can...
See all the beautiful horizons turn to intimate sunsets.

You can...
Tell me your worries, your troubles, your secrets
And I will listen with heart content.
You are a dreamer, a wisher,
Let me be your genie!
Just ask me girl and you shall receive.
Hmm... girl I'm all you need!

If I could stop time
with my words, my rhymes...
we could spend eternity in happiness.

You say you love this, you say you that,
I say I just want you to come back
Into your life and into mine. Don't get me wrong
I love what you are doing and making a living for yourself
But stop take a rest and enjoy the love your friends...
Have for you, like me for instance.
I don't know the game or how to play it
I only know that over the years as I...

Saw you, talked to you, I like you.
You went from a smart and pretty girl in my class
To a fine and intelligent young lady
Whom I consider as a friend!
I know I can't help you with everything
(everyone tries to remind me, I'm only human
and that I can only do so much!)
but I will be there when I can, spirit and all.
Your guardian angel, just give me a call!
Share your troubles and problems and your fears,
I'll do my best to comfort and take away your tears!

If I could stop time
With my words, my rhymes…
I would tell you my wishes, my dreams.

Let you know how I feel…
What I think of the world.
I would share my joys and hide my sorrows.

If I could do anything
With my words and my rhymes…
I would ask you to be mine
And show you a good time.

Oh, if I could only stop time!

Drama

She works hard until the very end,
A loving, caring, special friend.
Its just that she has this crush
A young man who gives her heart a rush.
She tells me how much she loves him
And I say why not ask him then.
Ask him, will you be mine
Because you are so fine.
She gives me a look, like it's the end of the world,
Telling me how this boy runs after this slutty girl.
Then to top off the problems in her life,
She tells me of her family and her friend's strife.
Her friend also works hard through and through
But when these girls don't talk they turn blue.
So, I try and help by giving one a clue,
Saying "hey your best friend really misses you!"
So they talk and catch up and have a little fun
And the next day when I saw her,
Her smile was brighter than the sun.
But then the happiness came to a blur
Because her parents were torn
And her broken heart was worn.
I thought to myself, it seems so wrong
For anyone to go through pain so strong.
I told her to have hope in her heart
And that her dreams won't fall apart.
Then the thought of that boy begins to tease
Her again,
And I'm thinking of how to ease
Her pain as a friend.
I could talk to him and let the secret slip
But if it doesn't work she'll give me a lot of lip.

Me

When I look in the mirror, what do I see?
Confusion, emotion, and plenty of curiosity.
A boy who only knows protection,
Safe in a world striving for perfection.
When I look in the mirror, I see
Those brown eyes looking at me,
Searching, thinking, hoping to see
What lays ahead. Will it be
Plenty of joy, drama, friends or sorrow?
I'll just have to wait for tomorrow.
Still what makes me, me?
Does everyone see what I see?
Who am I, some poor little boy seeking answers?
How come it just can't be fair?
Sometimes I look and I just don't care.

In the house my family shares
Along the walls, in the halls, are…
Pictures of a boy whose eyes shine like stars.
I try to remember his thoughts, my thought…
At the time of the flash
But all I know is that the years fly by fast.
When I look in the mirror, what do I see?
Hmmm…. Looks like jealousy?
I may have it good but I don't give it credit.
Every friend I had ever met,
Has worked hard, pushing past their limit.
Refusing to even think to quit
And here we have all we need,
Success with only one mouth to feed.
Yet still… when I look in the mirror, I see
Who longs to live for eternity,
To see if true peace will ever come
To a dramatic cold world where there is none.
I've seen pain beyond my small experience.
I've only had a small hit there,
A little fall here.
But compared to a bullet piercing the chest,
Laying a smoking body on the street to rest,
My small skirmishes mean nothing in life
To anyone who has only known strife.
Looking harder at that mirror, I see

A foolish boy who makes mistakes easily.
A boy driven by joy and glee,
Who thinks he has no one and feels lonely.
Yet, in reality
I have friends who think of me,
Who I can talk to
Whenever I feel sad and blue.
We are truly partners in this world… me and you.
Live, thrive and succeed is all we can do.
As I've looked at this mirror over the years
I've watched my smiles and tears.
Like every true human, I never notice how
Life or rather time goes so quickly when you are having fun
And how miserable people are with regrets than those with none.
Right now, I am looking at the mirror,
Want to know what I see?
This boy, this young man, I like to call me! D, O, N, A, L, D

Rain

When it's the calm, quiet mist
I just watch and listen.
I try to forget my worries, my troubles.
With each drop that hits the pane,
I let go of my stress, my pain.
Before the lightning, before the thunder,
I just look out the window and wonder
"What are they doing, are they okay?"
I don't know why I get this way
When I see or think a friend is in need.
I want to be the umbrella
As the clouds grow gray and begins to bleed.
Yeah I like the rainy mist
When I get sad like this.
But when it begins to pour and pour
I can't help but think of my friends once more.
Like each drop of a tormenting storm,
We all fall down in our special way.
Some fall short, some change their form,
As the rain speeds up, shooting down in a rush.
I feel, I hear their busy hearts pulse.
I wonder again, can I truly be their umbrella,
Protecting them, comforting them.
I wish I could… and
If I had the power I would.

A Mother's Day

It has almost been eighteen years
Yet still you remain kind and dear.
Even when we are no where near,
Our safety is still your greatest fear.

But hey guess what! Today is the day…
Where all mothers get to have their way.
No cooking, no cleaning, put that broom away.
We can take you out or let you rest where you stay.

Just do what you want on this special day
And like "always" we will do what you say,
Loving and caring for you in our own special way!

Ebony

Pure, strong and undying
Is this friendship underlying
The cool quiet mask of the girl in the corner.
No she is not a mute, a shy girl, or a mourner.
Just a good friend thats all,
Who loves to say hey when I see her in the hall.
Even though I just really met her this fall

Hope

The palest sunlight, hides even the darkest storm.
In a icy cold blizzard a blanket can keep you warm.
I know the saddest days start and seem to never end
But then you get a "hey, whats up" from a good friend
And looking back on the pain, the suffering, the trouble,
Its not so bad now that we will never be apart.
When you're tired, hungry, lost, sad
Unhappy, scared, or just plain mad,
Take a look there and you will find
It is all just in your mind.
The rain, the thunder, the lightning, the hail
None of it doesn't matter if you are willing to prevail.
The palest sunlight, stops even the darkest storm.
In a freezing blizzard, a blanket will keep you warm.
Thinking there is a chance, a possibility
Is the first step to making a dream a reality.
They used to say the more you believe
The more you can achieve.
I say if you are willing to breathe
You should be able to succeed!

Donald Thompson II is currently a college student, majoring in mathematics. Poetry, tutoring, and bike riding are some of his hobbies. Through his family and friends Donald lives to see a day where peace is more than a dream in this cruel, cold world. As a start towards this better future he assists his classmates, forms study groups, and participate in various volunteer and community service events.

www.ingramcontent.com/pod-product-compliance
Lightning Source LLC
Chambersburg PA
CBHW021912040426
42447CB00007B/824